For a better life
Truth

A Book on Self-Empowerment

Compiled by
M. M. Walia

NEW DAWN PRESS, INC.
USA• UK• INDIA

NEW DAWN PRESS GROUP

Published by New Dawn Press Group
New Dawn Press, Inc., 244 South Randall Rd # 90, Elgin, IL 60123
e-mail: sales@newdawnpress.com

New Dawn Press, 2 Tintern Close, Slough, Berkshire, SL1-2TB, UK
e-mail: salesuk@newdawnpress.org

New Dawn Press (An Imprint of Sterling Publishers (P) Ltd)
A-59, Okhla Industrial Area, Phase-II, New Delhi-110020, India
e-mail: info@sterlingpublishers.com
www.sterlingpublishers.com

For a better life – Truth

© 2006, Sterling Publishers (P) Ltd
ISBN 1 84557 582 2

All rights are reserved. No part of this publication may be reproduced, stored in a retrieval system or transmitted, in any form or by any means, mechanical, photocopying, recording or otherwise, without prior written permission of the publisher.

PRINTED IN INDIA

This is Truth

Truth liberates;
Truth is power;
Truth is freedom.
It's the lamp
that illuminates the heart,
dispels doubt and darkness.
The effulgence of God is truth.
Welcome God into your heart.
– Sri Sathya Sai Baba

Life
is a perennial
search for truth.
— *Yajur Veda*

Truth

is the foundation
of real spirituality,
and courage is its soul.
— *Sri Aurobindo*

Mahatma Gandhi on Truth

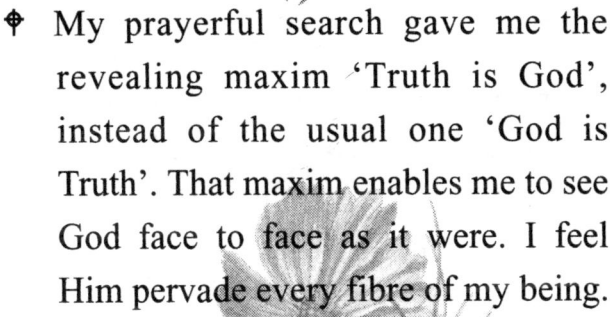

- My prayerful search gave me the revealing maxim 'Truth is God', instead of the usual one 'God is Truth'. That maxim enables me to see God face to face as it were. I feel Him pervade every fibre of my being.

- And then we have another thing in Hindu philosophy, viz., God alone is and nothing else exists, and the same truth you find emphasised in the

Kalma of Islam — that God alone is and 'nothing else exists.' In fact, the Sanskrit word for Truth is a word which literally means that which exists — *Sat*. So I have come to the conclusion that the definition: 'Truth is God', gives me the greatest satisfaction.

What then is Truth?

- A difficult question, but I have solved it for myself by saying that it is what the voice within tells you.

- We should understand the word *Satya* or Truth in a wide sense. There should be Truth in thought, Truth in speech, and Truth in action. To the man who has realised this Truth in its fullness, nothing else remains to be known, because all knowledge is necessarily included in it.

✽ The quest of Truth involves — self-suffering, sometimes even unto death. There can be no place in it for even a trace of self-interest. In such a selfless search for Truth nobody can lose his bearing for long. Directly he takes to the right path. Therefore the pursuit of Truth is true *bhakti* (devotion).

✽ The word *Satya* (Truth) is derived from *Sat*, which means 'being'. Nothing is or exists in reality except Truth. That is why *Sat* or Truth is perhaps the most important name of

God. In fact, it is more correct to say that Truth is God, than to say that God is Truth. But as we cannot do without a ruler, such names for God as 'King of Kings' or 'The Almighty' will remain. In a deeper sense, however, it will be realised, that *Sat* or *Satya* is the only correct and fully significant name for God.

✣ And where there is Truth, there is also knowledge which is true. That is why the word *Chit* or knowledge is associated with the name of God. And where there is true knowledge, there is always bliss (*ananda*). Hence, we know God as *Sat-Chit-Ananda*, One who combines in Himself truth, knowledge and bliss.

✛ Devotion to the Truth is the sole justification for our existence. All our activities should be centred on Truth. Truth should be the very breath of our life. When once this stage in the pilgrim's progress is reached, all other rules of correct living will come without effort, and obedience to them will be instinctive. But without Truth it is impossible to observe any principles or rules in life.

✢ Truth is not truth merely because it is ancient. Nor is it necessarily to be regarded with suspicion, because it is ancient. There are some fundamentals of life which may not be lightly given up because they are difficult to enforce in one's life.

✢ Human life is a series of compromises and it is not always easy to achieve in practice what one has found to be true in theory. There are eternal principles which admit no compromise and one must be prepared to lay down one's life in the practice of them.

✥ The pursuit of Truth is true (devotion). It is the path that leads to God, and, therefore, there is no place in it for cowardice, no place for defeat. It is the talisman by which death itself becomes the portal to life eternal.

✟ From the standpoint of pure Truth, the body too is a possession. It has been truly said, that desires for enjoyment creates bodies for the soul. When this desire vanishes, there remains no further need for the body, and man is free from the vicious circle of birth and death.

✟ How beautiful it would be, if all of us, men and women, devoted ourselves wholly to Truth in all that we might do in our waking hours, whether working, eating, drinking or playing, till dissolution of the body makes us one with Truth?

✤ Our life is a long and arduous quest for Truth, and the soul requires inward restfulness to attain its full height.

✤ Proneness to exaggerate, to suppress or modify the truth wittingly or unwittingly, is a natural weakness of man.

✠ If we had attained the full vision of Truth, we would no longer be mere seekers, but would have become one with God, for Truth is God.

Gems of Wisdom from Sri Sathya Sai Baba

"Truth will always triumph; do not doubt that in the least."

❖ Everything has been created out of truth and all creation is embedded in truth.

❖ Truth is all-embracing and integrating and it sees no distinction. Truth is the current and love is the bulb it has to illumine. Through truth you can experience love and through love you can visualise truth.

❖ Adhere to the truth; that is the surest means of removing fear from your heart.

❖ Truth is a fundamental principle. All religions have declared that man should honour his pledges. This was the primary teaching of the great law-giver Manu.

❖ In the Vedas these three qualities have been described as *Sathyam, Sivam, Sundaram*. Thus, though different words are used, their essential meaning is the same. Spiritual discipline consists in recognising the unity underlying the apparent diversity and realising divinity.

❖ God is the embodiment of Truth. Speak the truth; speak what is pleasing.

- ❖ Speak the truth and practice dharma. There is no better stabilising factor in society, no more support for individual progress than truth *(satya)*.

- ❖ Truth cannot be made and marred.

- ❖ The permanent and eternal truth of God should be the ultimate aim.

- ❖ You cannot hide truth for a long time. However, much you may try to hide, the truth will always come out.

❖ Implementing truth into action is dharma. There is no dharma higher than truth.

❖ The search for truth is essential for the realisation of God.

❖ God is the embodiment of truth. Speak the truth; speak what is pleasing. Do not utter a truth that is unpleasant.

❖ Truth is something that is not modified by time or space or *guna* (attribute). It must be the same forever, unaffected and unchanged. It should not be proved false by some subsequent event or knowledge.

- ❖ Have faith that truth will save you in the long run. Stick to it, regardless of what might befall.

- ❖ Speak the truth and speak pleasantly. If speaking the truth will cause grief or pain, keep silent.

❖ Truth is one's real nature and when you are yourself, there comes a great flood of joy welling up within you.

❖ When you deny yourself and deceive yourself, shame darkens your mind and breeds fear. You take the path of falsehood because of the passions of lust, greed, hate, pride.

❖ Contentment, humility, detachment — these keep you on the path of Truth.

❖ Believe that Love is God, Truth is God, Love is Truth, Truth is Love.

❖ For it is only when there is love that you have no fear. And fear is the Mother of falsehood. If you have no fear, you will adhere to Truth.

*That which never changes
and is unrestricted by
anything, is Truth.*

*Truth is beauty

and beauty is Truth.*

❖ Harmlessness, mercy, character, control over senses, peace, courage and humility are the virtues which a seeker of truth should possess.

❖ Discrimination between the 'seer' and the 'seen' is the road leading to the realisation of Truth.

❖ A sour truth is better than a sweet lie.

The nearer one approaches Truth,
the happier one becomes.
For the essential nature of
Truth is Absolute Bliss.

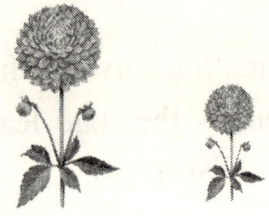

Truth is noble and sweet;
Truth can deliver you from evil.
There is no saviour in the
world except the truth.

— *The Buddha*

Trustfulness- A State of Inner Opening

- An important condition is a childlike trust.

- To aspire is indispensable. But some people aspire with such a conflict inside them between faith and absence of faith, trust and distrust, between the optimism which is sure of victory and a pessimism which asks itself when the catastrophe will come.

- Now if this is in the being, you may aspire, but you do not get anything. And this is because you demolish your aspirations all the time by your lack of confidence.

- But if you truly have trust — all turns out well.

When one aspires for the Force, when one asks the Divine for help, if one asks with the unshakable certitude that it will come, that it is impossible that it will not, then it is sure to come. And some people are constantly in this state of trustfulness. When there is something to be received, they are always there to receive it. There are others, when there is something to be received, a force descends, and they are always closed at that moment.

And it is strange, is it not, that outwardly there is no difference between people who trust and those who do not? The people who do not may have exactly the same goodwill, the same aspiration, the same wish to do good. But those who have this smiling confidence within them, do not question, do not ask themselves whether they will have it or not have it, whether the divine will answer or not — the question does not arise, it is something understood. They feel:

"What I need will be given to me; if I pray I shall have an answer; if I am in difficulty and ask for help, will come — and not only will it come but it will manage everything."

If the trust is there, spontaneous, candid, unquestioning, it works better than anything else, and the results are marvellous. It is with the contradictions and doubts of the mind that one spoils everything.

By doubting, one builds a wall between oneself and the force one wants to receive. The psychic being has this trust, has it wonderfully, without a shadow, without an argument, without a contradiction. And when it is like that, there is not a prayer which does not get an answer, no aspiration which is not realised.

At every moment all the unforeseen, the unexpected, the unknown is before us — and what happens to us depends

mostly on the intensity and purity of our faith.

— *The Mother*

Truth is God

✟ An ethical life is based upon discrimination between truth and falsehood. Just as the pearl is retained while the shell is discarded, the essence which is Truth must be accepted and the non-essential rejected. Then again, individual exertion and Divine Grace should both be existent. One should also constantly remember that the *body* and the *soul* are separate. This is a highly beneficial exercise. It is indispensable for realising the Truth, the Truth that persists in creation, existence and destruction — the Truth which is God Himself.

☥ In everything that you do, use all the strength and talent with which you are endowed, speaking and acting truthfully. At first, you might fail in this and you might encounter difficulties and suffering. But, ultimately, you are bound to succeed and achieve victory and bliss.

✣ Life's principle within each of us is the truth. We would not be existent without it and once we are not there, the world also ceases. This life principle is identified as the human soul which in turn is the 'resident divinity' within each individual. It is this truth which is the basis of every other thing and with the power of which the heart beats, the lungs breathe and the system works. The role of the human intellect is to find out the Truth.

- Interestingly, when one realises and experiences this Truth, one sees that the same Truth pervades every other person and object. And in essence we are all one.

- Truth has different levels. There is the truth of sense perception such as, 'the fire burns'. One can ascertain this with one's senses. There is also the truth by inference, such as 'man is mortal'. We base this statement on the strength of our observation of those around us and extend it to arrive at a general conclusion even though we may not have seen every human being born in this world dying. Apart from all these is the Truth which is incapable of being destroyed or hurt. It persists and pervades the whole Cosmos.

— ***The Stream of Divine Love***
Sri Sathya Sai Baba

*Whatever scriptures one may study,
whatever sadhanas one may practise
or pilgrimages one may make,
unless one succeeds
in getting rid of the impurities
in the heart,
life will remain worthless
and meaningless.
Purification of the heart
is the essence of all scriptural teachings
and the basic goal of life.*
—Sri Sathya Sai Baba

Truth Orientation

❖ Truth is that which abides forever.

❖ The search for Truth is not limited to any particular religious frame or pattern, for nature gives mute intimation of Truth to every mortal — in the depths of his heart.

❖ Follow the path of Truth with maximum effort. There are many along this arduous road, who would misdirect you.

- ❖ To seek Truth is to pass through an ordeal, hard and painful. But the ordeal ends in real joy.

- ❖ The intellect will never become pure unless the mind is directed towards and fixed upon Truth.

- ❖ Truthfulness (in behaviour) implies that one always be truthful in speech, honest and straightforward in action, and free from sin.

Sublime Association

- ❖ It is through sublime association that one is able to discriminate between that which IS (Truth) from that which is NOT (Untruth) and to recognise what is good and what is evil.
- ❖ It is through this that one achieves real peace.
- ❖ One acquires the disposition of right thought, right belief and right endeavour by participating in sublime association.

Meditation on the True Name

❖ Remembrance of the ever-existent (God) sanctifies human existence; it liberates man from the clutches of rebirth; it cools the fire of desire, and it gives that comfort which is imperishable.

❖ It is the reflection/concentration upon Truth which destroys all sins and leads to the vision of God.

❖ Listen to spiritual teaching as the essence of all saints and seers. They all suggest worship of one True Element, though the methods are diverse.

Righteousness

❖ Firmness in righteous conduct is achieved only through consistent dedication to the Truth.

❖ Deepen your love for the person who falls from a principle (stumbles from the path of Truth). Lift him up through your intense love.

❖ The authentic meaning of life is to be found in the reflection on *Samata Tattva* (the fundamental Truth).

— *Mahatma Mangat Ram*

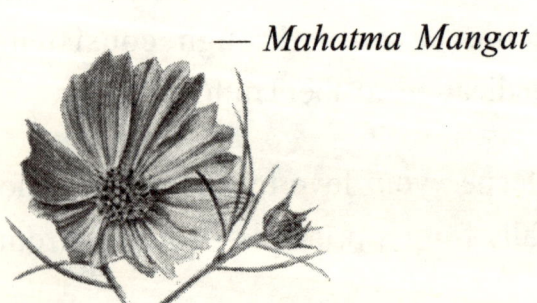

A word or action, which does not make others unhappy or injures their feelings – that kind of action is called Truth. It depends upon the intention and not on the action.

A lie which benefits others – that is the real Truth.

— *Swami Visudha Chaitanya*

Constant devotion to spiritual knowledge, realisation of the essence of Truth, this is declared to be wisdom; what is opposed to this is ignorance.

— *The Bhagavad Gita*

Truth in thought,
Truth in speech,
Truth in action.

To the man who has realised this Truth in perfection, nothing else remains to be known, because all knowledge is necessarily included in it. What is not included in it is not the Truth and therefore not true knowledge; and there can be no inward peace without true knowledge. If we once learn how to apply this never-failing test of truth, we will at once be able to find out what is worth seeing and what is worth reading.

The quest of Truth involves — self-suffering, sometimes even unto death. There can be no place in it for even a trace of self-interest. In such selfless search for Truth nobody can lose his bearings for long. Sometimes one takes to the wrong path, one stumbles and through the power of truth is thus redirected to the right path. Therefore the pursuit of Truth is true devotion. It is the path that leads to God and, therefore, there is no place in it for cowardice, no place for defeat. It is the talisman by which death itself becomes the portal to life eternal.

Experience has taught us that silence is part of a spiritual discipline. A tendency to exaggerate, to suppress or modify the truth wittingly or unwittingly, is a natural weakness in man, and silence is necessary in order to surmount it. A man of few words will rarely be thoughtless in his speech; he will measure every word.

— *Mahatma Gandhi*

> When they listen to that which has been revealed unto the Messenger, you see their eyes overflow with tears because of their recognition of the Truth. They say, "Our Lord, we believe. Inscribe us as among the witnesses."
>
> – The Qur'an

Falsehood shall be destroyed;
Truth in the end shall prevail

—Adi Granth

Realisation of Truth
is higher than all else;
Higher still is truthful living.

—Adi Granth

Sri Aurobindo on Truth

If you want to be an instrument of Truth you must always speak the truth and not indulge in falsehood. But this does not mean that you must speak everything to everybody. To conceal the truth by silence or refusal to speak is permissible, because the truth may be misunderstood or misused by those who are not prepared for it or who are opposed to it — it can even be made the starting point for distortion or falsehood. But to speak falsehood is another matter. Even in jest it should be avoided, because it tends to lower the consciousness.

The last point is again from the highest standpoint — the truth as one knows it in the mind is not enough, for the ideas in the mind may be erroneous or insufficient — it is necessary to have true knowledge in one's consciousness.

It is not necessary to leave the earth to find the Truth; it is not necessary to leave life to find one's soul; it is not necessary to give up the world in order to enter into the Divine world. The Divine is everywhere, in everything, and He is not hidden ... it is because we do not take the trouble to discover Him.

The Certitude of Truth

❖ There is an inner reality — within ourselves, within the earth, within the Universe — and we, the earth and the Universe exist only as a function of this truth, and if it did not exist, we would not last. And because truth is the real basis of the Universe, naturally it is this which will triumph;

and all that opposes this cannot endure as long as this does, because it is That, the eternal thing which is at the base of the Universe.

❖ One must remember, the certitude of Truth's final history.

— *The Mother*

The Vedantic Message of Truth

❖ The knowledge of the truth of the Atman, the immortal Self of man, is the basis of true religion, as understood in the Vedanta. The more spiritual a person, the more fearless he is, and the more gentle and compassionate. These are the fruits of the knowledge of Truth.

Love of Truth

❖ Truth (*satya*), which expresses itself as righteousness (*dharma*) in human life, is an eternal value. It cannot be moulded and shaped to suit human convenience. The latter, on the other hand, must be made to conform to Truth. The mind and heart of Nachiketa had become fearless because of his love of truth. Even death held no terror for him. He is a shining example for human society, ancient or modern.

Truth does not pay homage to any society, ancient or modern. Society has to pay homage to Truth, or die. Societies should be moulded according to the truth, and truth should not adjust itself to society. That society is the greatest, where the highest truths become practical. That is my opinion; and if society is not fit for the highest truths, make it so; and the sooner, the better.

Spiritual Boldness

❖ The sun cannot dry, fire cannot burn, the sword cannot kill, for I am the birthless, the deathless, the ever living, omnipotent, omnipresent spirit." This is spiritual boldness. Stand up, men and women, in this spirit, dare to believe in the Truth, dare to practise the Truth! The world requires a few hundred bold men and women.

❖ Practise that boldness which dares to know the Truth, which dares to show the Truth in life, which does not quake before death, nay, welcomes it and makes man know that he is the Spirit; that in the whole universe, nothing can kill him.

Morality

❖ Truth, purity, and unselfishness — wherever these are present, there is no power below or above the sun to crush the possessor thereof. Equipped with these, one individual is able to face the whole universe in opposition.

The Test of Truth

❖ "And here is the test of truth: anything that makes you weak — physically, intellectually and spiritually — reject as poison; there is no life in it; it cannot be true. Truth is strengthening, Truth is purity, Truth is all knowledge."

Advaita - The Truth

❖ The Lord is the creation. The physical creation is He. The thoughts are also the Lord. The consciousness behind the creation, behind the thoughts is *satya*, the Truth, which is also the truth of the Lord. Until this truth is discovered, I need an altar where I can place my head and invoke the Lord, the almighty, the all-powerful, the all-knowledgeable.

❖ I worship the Lord who is everything and then I discover the fact that I am everything, this is *advaita*. *Advaita* is the fact; it is the Truth, which cannot be shaken by anybody, nor can it be improved upon by anyone.

❖ No one can tell me that his God is more than limitless. On the other hand, we cannot accept that a Lord is less than limitless because it is against the experience of life. Until you are free from limitations, you will never rest content. Like the river finding her level, until she reaches the ocean, she cannot rest content.

She cannot reconcile that there is a dam, and that she need not flow any further. She keeps on exerting her pressure on the dam, she raises her level and does whatever is necessary until she can flow further, until she can continue her journey to the ocean. Thus she goes on all the time, because until the river reaches the ocean, until she has a vision of the ocean, the flow does not stop. Understand, that the river has to lose her name and form.

— **His Gospel of Man-making**
Swami Vivekananda

- ❖ *"Truth obtains victory, not untruth. Truth is the way that leads to the regions of light. Sages travel therein free from desires and reach the supreme abode of Truth."*
- ❖ *"This Atman is attained by truth and tapas whence comes true wisdom and chastity. The wise who strive and who are pure, see him within the body in his pure glory and light."*
- ❖ *"Truth is victorious, never untruth. Truth is the way; truth is the goal of life, reached by sages who are free from self-will."*

– Mundaka Upanishad

Truth - The Ultimate Power

- ❖ In Indian scriptures, the practice of Truth has been accorded great significance since ancient times. In the *Mahabharata*, Truth has been accorded an interesting connotation. "*Satyam Bhuthitam Paroktam*", which means, *Let every one prosper*; to speak thus, is the ultimate truth.

- ❖ Some great men of the past have made truth the very basis of their lives. Raja Harish Chandra, Yudhishter and in the recent past Mahatma Gandhi are some well known examples of such people.

❖ When seen from the material and spiritual points of view, the word Truth has varied manifestations. From the mundane standpoint, Truth has a restricted meaning, but Truth has actually very deep connotations. The word Truth tends to be interpreted differently from time to time at different levels of consciousness.

However, since in the final analysis, the Ultimate Truth is God Himself, there can, in fact, be no two definitions of Truth.

❖ Brahman — the eternal transcendental reality is the only Truth; everything else is unreal.

❖ Divine attributes such as Truth (*Satya*), Non-violence (*Ahimsa*), Knowledge (*Gyan*) are subservient to only the supremely realised or God-heads. These qualities can only be imbibed through their blessings and by following their dictates.

❖ Adamant adherence to truthfulness in day-to-day living, irrespective of its consequences, cannot always be sanctified, more so, when rigidly sticking to the truth is aimed at acquiring fame as a great truthful personality. In fact, it has been beautifully put — a truthful person is not one who always tells the Truth but whose utterance always becomes true!

❖ The finest commentary on Truth has been given by Lord Swaminarayana in Vachanamritam. He says:

"When the saint, who is in rapport with God, pronounces before the cardinal Truth: "You are separate from body, *indriyas* and *pranas*, and are the eternal *Atman* — the knower, and the body and the appendages to the body are all perishable", he irrevocably accepts this Truth and behaves as *Atman* but never responds to the frivolous calls of the mind.

"Such a devotee carefully discards contact with such persons or such sense-objects which are likely to deter him from the path of spiritual ascent. He accepts only eternal truths and rejects untruth."

— *Swami Mukundjeevandas*

Truthfulness

❖ Truthfulness consists mainly in uttering a thought as it is actually perceived. Ordinarily, a liar is one who does not have the moral courage to express what he sincerely feels. This disparity between thought and words creates in his mind a habit to entertain a sort of "self-cancellation" of thoughts. This impoverishes the individual's mental strength, will power, and dynamism. Such an exhausted mental character is too weak, thereafter to make any progress in life's pilgrimage.

❖ Truthfulness in its essential meaning is not merely giving a verbal expression to one's honest feeling, but in its deeper import it is the attunement of one's mental thoughts to his or her intellectual convictions.

❖ Unless we are ready to discipline and marshal our thought-forces to the unquestioning authority of our own reason, chastened with knowledge in the ensuing chaos within, we cannot grow to realise our true and divine nature.

—*Swami Chinmayananda*

Earth is round;
Earth moves;
Not seen, but true.
Sky is blue;
Sunset is golden;
Seen, but false.
Energy in the atom;
Vitality in the sun;
Gravitational force;
Not seen, but true.
Double moon;
Mirage waters;
Dreams and hallucinations;
Seen, but false.
World we see, but not true.
Truth we see not, but true.
— *Swami Chinmayananda*

H H The Dalai Lama on Truth

❖ Truth is the best guarantor and the real foundation of freedom and democracy. It does not matter whether you are weak or strong or whether your cause has many or few adherents; truth will still prevail.

❖ Though in the past, the simple expression of truth has usually been dismissed as unrealistic, these last few years have proved that it is an immense force in the human mind and, as a result, in the shaping of history.

The Four Noble Truths

- ❖ The existence of sorrow
- ❖ The cause of sorrow
- ❖ The cessation of sorrow
- ❖ The way which leads to the cessation of sorrow

The root of Buddhist doctrine is the four noble truths— true sufferings, sources, cessations and paths. The four truths are two groups of effect and cause: sufferings and their sources; and cessations of sufferings and the paths for actualising those cessations. Suffering is like an illness; the external and internal conditions that bring about the illness are the sources of suffering. The state of cure from the illness is the cessation of suffering and of its cause. The medicine that cures the disease is the path of truth.

❖ Truth is best as it is. No one can alter it; neither can anyone improve upon it. Have faith in truth and live it.

❖ Truth is noble and sweet; truth can deliver you from evil. There is no saviour in the world except the truth.

No man should blindly follow his ancestors.
Nay, each must see with his own eyes, hear with
his own ears and investigate truth himself...
If only men could search out truth,
they would find themselves united.

In order to find the truth we must give up our
prejudices, our own small trivial notions; an open
and receptive mind is essential – Silence must be
accepted. No truth can contradict another truth. A
light is good in whatever lamp it is burning.

– Baha'u'llah

Eternal Values

❖ There is no virtue higher than Truth, there is no sin greater than falsehood; therefore should man seek protection under Truth with all his soul.

—Mahanirvana Tantra

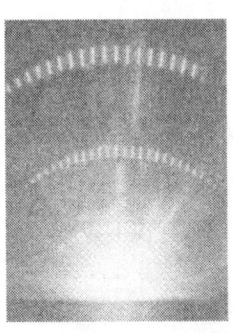

❖ *He is true in the truest sense of the word who is true in word, in thought, and in deed.*

— *Anonymous*

❖ *Say what is true, even if it is bitter and displeasing to you.*

— *Mohammed*

❖ *Unite and make common cause with all agencies that fight for truth.*

—Zarathushtra

❖ *It takes two of us to discover Truth:*
One to utter it; and
One to understand it.

❖ *Many a doctrine is like a windowpane. We see through it, but it divides us from truth.*

❖ *A truth is to be known always, to be uttered sometimes.*

*An exaggeration
is a Truth
that has lost its temper.*

*He who listens
to the Truth
is not less than
he who utters the Truth.*

*If you can see
only what light reveals,
and hear
only what the soul announces,
then, in Truth,
you do not see, nor do you hear.*

Truth

is like all beautiful things

in the world;

it does not disclose its desirability

except to those who first feel the influence of falsehood.

— *Kahlil Gibran*

❖ That which never changes and is unrestricted by anything, is Truth.

❖ Truth defies definition as a metaphysical entity.

❖ Truth Absolute can be that which is one without a second, and non-dual and homogenous.

❖ Mercy, character, control over the senses, peace, courage and humility are the virtues which a seeker of Truth should possess.

- *Discrimination between the 'seer' and the 'seen' is the road leading to the realisation of Truth.*

- *The nearer one approaches the truth, the happier one becomes. For the essential nature of Truth is positive—Absolute Bliss.*

- *A sour truth is better than a sweet lie.*

- *Untruth is a lesser truth. Evil is a lesser degree of goodness.*

— Swami Sivananda

Can Truth be Defined?

❖ It is not easy to define Truth. A simple definition of Truth can be –

"What is not subject to negation is Truth."

❖ What is not subject to negation, in all the three periods of time is Truth. Because everything else is subject to negation and does not qualify to be called 'satya'.

– Swami Dayanandji